Big Pop
Instrumental Solos

Published 2003
© International Music Publications Limited
Griffin House 161 Hammersmith Road London England W6 8BS

Project management Artemis Music Limited

Contents

All By Myself

Words and Music by Eric Carmen and Sergei Rachmaninoff

All The Way

Words by Sammy Cahn
Music by Jimmy Van Heusen

Arthur's Theme

Words and Music by Peter Allen, Burt Bacharach, Christopher Cross and Carole Bayer Sager

Amazed

Words and Music by Marv Green, Aimee Mayo and Chris Lindsey

Anakin's Theme
(from *Star Wars Episode 1: The Phantom Menace*)

Music by John Williams

Angels

Words and Music by Robert Williams and Guy Chambers

As Time Goes By

Words and Music by Herman Hupfeld

Beat It

Words and Music by Michael Jackson

Bad

Words and Music by Michael Jackson

Beautiful Stranger

Words and Music by Madonna Ciccone and William Orbit

19

Beyond The Sea (La Mer)

Original Words and Music by Charles Trenet and Albert Lasry
English Words by Jack Lawrence

Billie Jean

Words and Music by Michael Jackson

Blueberry Hill

Words and Music by Al Lewis, Vincent Rose and Larry Stock

Can't Get You Out Of My Head

Words and Music by Cathy Dennis and Robert Davis

Careless Whisper

Words and Music by George Michael and Andrew Ridgeley

Days Of Wine And Roses

Words by Johnny Mercer
Music by Henry Mancini

Theme From *Cheers*

Words by Judy Angelo
Music by Gary Portnoy

Don't It Make My Brown Eyes Blue

Words and Music by Richard Leigh

Moderately slow swing ♩ = 84

rit.

Duel Of The Fates
(from *Star Wars Episode 1: The Phantom Menace*)

Music by John Williams

Maestoso, with great force (♩ = 44)

Allegro (♩ = 152)

Evergreen

Words and Music by Barbra Streisand and Paul Williams

Eternal Flame

Words and Music by Billy Steinberg, Tom Kelly and Susannah Hoffs

Family Affair

Words and Music by Sylvester Stewart

Repeat and fade

Flying Without Wings

Words and Music by Steve Mac and Wayne Hector

rit.

Genie In A Bottle

Words and Music by Pam Sheyne, David Frank and Steve Kipner

Great Balls Of Fire

Words and Music by Jack Hammer and Otis Blackwell

The Greatest Love Of All

Words by Linda Creed
Music by Michael Masser

Handbags & Gladrags

Words and Music by Mike D'Abo

Hey, Good Lookin'

Words and Music by Hank Williams

The House Of The Rising Sun

Traditional
Arranged by Alan Price

Slow rock ♩ = 60

mp

mf

How Do I Live

Words and Music by Diane Warren

I Could Have Danced All Night
(from *My Fair Lady*)

Words by Alan Jay Lerner
Music by Frederick Loewe

I Don't Want To Miss A Thing

Words and Music by Diane Warren

I Say A Little Prayer

Words by Hal David
Music by Burt Bacharach

Just The Two Of Us

Words and Music by Ralph MacDonald, William Salter and Bill Withers

La Isla Bonita

Words and Music by Madonna Ciccone, Bruce Gaitsch and Patrick Leonard

D.C. al Coda

Coda

2

Livin' La Vida Loca

Words and Music by Robi Rosa and Desmond Child

Misty

Music by Errol Garner

My Heart Will Go On

Words by Will Jennings
Music by James Horner

Theme From *New York, New York*

Words by Fred Ebb
Music by John Kander

Oh, Pretty Woman

Words and Music by Roy Orbison and Bill Dees

Nothing's Gonna Change My Love For You

Words and Music by Michael Masser and Gerry Goffin

On Green Dolphin Street

Words by Ned Washington
Music by Bronislaw Kaper

On My Own

Words and Music by Carole Bayer Sager and Burt Bacharach

Over The Rainbow

Words by E Y Harburg
Music by Harold Arlen

Papa Don't Preach

Words and Music by Brian Elliot

The Pink Panther

Music by Henry Mancini

(We're Gonna) Rock Around The Clock

Words and Music by Jimmy De Knight and Max Freedman

The Rose

Words and Music by Amanda McBroom

Something About The Way You Look Tonight

Music by Elton John
Words by Bernie Taupin

Saving All My Love For You

Words by Gerry Goffin
Music by Michael Masser

Repeat and fade

Smooth

Words and Music by Itaal Shur and Robert Thomas

Moderate latin rock

"St. Elmo's Fire (Man In Motion)"

Words and Music by David Foster and John Parr

Star Wars (Main Theme)

Music by John Williams

Still

Words and Music by Lionel Richie

Summertime

Music and Lyrics by George Gershwin, Du Bose Heyward, Dorothy Heyward and Ira Gershwin

Tell Him

Words and Music by Linda Thompson, David Foster and Walter Afanasieff

Time After Time

Words and Music by Robert Hyman and Cyndi Lauper

Tomorrow (from *Annie*)

Words by Martin Charnin
Music by Charles Strouse

Tonight I Celebrate My Love

Words and Music by Michael Masser and Gerry Goffin

When A Man Loves A Woman

Words and Music by Calvin Lewis and Andrew Wright

True Blue

Words and Music by Madonna Ciccone and Stephen Bray

The Way You Make Me Feel

Words and Music by Michael Jackson

Who's That Girl?

Words and Music by Madonna Ciccone and Patrick Leonard

Wipe Out

Words and Music by Bob Berryhill, Pat Connolly, James Fuller and Ronald Wilson

Wind Beneath My Wings

Words and Music by Larry Henley and Jeff Silbar

Without You

Words and Music by Pete Ham and Tom Evans